This Little Tiger book
belongs to:

_____

_____

_____

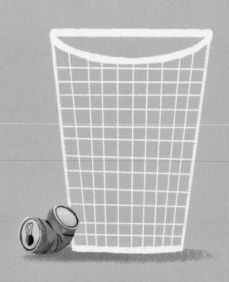

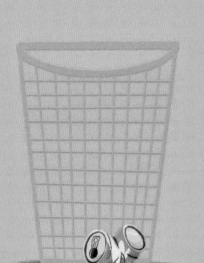

For Barb. Thanks for your
continued enthusiasm! ~ T C

For Olive ~ T N

LITTLE TIGER PRESS LTD,
an imprint of the Little Tiger Group
1 Coda Studios,
189 Munster Road,
London SW6 6AW
www.littletiger.co.uk

First published in Great Britain 2020
This edition published 2021
Text copyright © Tracey Corderoy 2020
Illustrations copyright © Tony Neal 2020
Tracey Corderoy and Tony Neal have asserted their rights
to be identified as the author and illustrator of this work
under the Copyright, Designs and Patents Act, 1988
A CIP catalogue record for this book is available
from the British Library

The Forest Stewardship Council® (FSC®) is an international,
non-governmental organisation dedicated to promoting responsible
management of the world's forests. FSC operates a system of forest
certification and product labelling that allows consumers to identify
wood and wood-based products from well-managed forests.

For more information about the FSC, please visit their website at www.fsc.org

IT'S ONLY ONE!

Tracey Corderoy

Tony Neal

LITTLE TIGER

LONDON

Sunnyville was perfect.
Friendly and fun.
It twinkled with total loveliness!

But then, without
thinking . . .

. . . Rhino did **this.**

But it wasn't.

DONK!

So **he** did this.

What? It's only one.

But – of course . . .

Wrong again!
Mouse couldn't believe her EARS.

This was simply **awful**.

Sunnyville had lost its twinkle completely.
And now EVERYONE was grumpy!

Then Mouse had an idea!

And she did this.

It was only one,
but . . .

It smelled just like the Sunnyville
they all remembered.

Now Rhino knew **exactly** what to do.

And wrapper by wrapper . . .

flower by flower . . .

. . . Sunnyville soon twinkled brighter than ever.

And everyone **LOVED** it.

Hooray!

A note from the author, Tracey Corderoy . . .

I live in a beautiful little valley and love the big green trees and twinkling stream. We have chocolate-coloured rabbits who hop through the fields. and little mice who scurry through the grass. Keeping it neat and a good place to be means that everyone can enjoy it. In our story. Rhino drops just one small wrapper. He thinks this will be ok. But – uh oh! – before he knows it. all his friends are doing just what **they** please too. and boy. is it noisy and messy! This story is about thinking of others so that everyone can be happy.

And the illustrator, Tony Neal . . .

Sometimes we might want to say, "It's only one!" But if we all dropped "only one" piece of rubbish, things would soon get a whole lot messier! Let's be clean, try to be green, and keep the places we live in looking great. We can do this by being thoughtful about our actions and the way we treat others. Let's look after this planet we live on – for we have only one!

Let's learn to be good neighbours!

Little acts of kindness make our neighbourhood a better place to live. Let's try to . . .
* smile and say "hello" when we meet our friends
* treat others as we would like to be treated
* look after the spaces we all share
* help those in need

Let's put our litter in the bin!

No one likes to look at rubbish. It can also be smelly, and harmful to both people and animals. Let's try to . . .
* carry our litter until we find the nearest bin
* take it home if we cannot find one nearby
* recycle our rubbish when we can

Let's make our park a happy place!

Everybody loves the park, so treat it with good care.
Let's try to . . .
* leave the flowers unpicked, so that everyone can enjoy them
* be kind and gentle to birds, squirrels, ducks and other wildlife
* share when we play on the swings or the slide

Let's learn from each other!

I'll help my neighbours!

I won't call people names.

Let's keep the noise down!

It can be fun to scream, shout and play music – but remember that others might prefer peace and quiet. Let's try to . . .

* be aware of other people when playing with our friends
* keep the volume low on our TVs and music systems
* tread lightly with our feet if others live below us

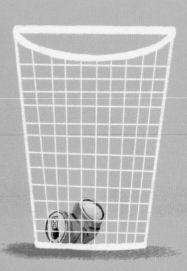
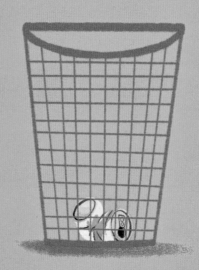
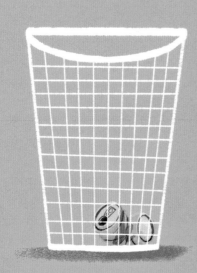

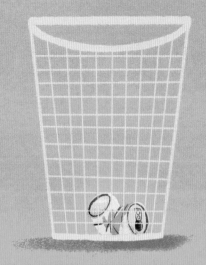

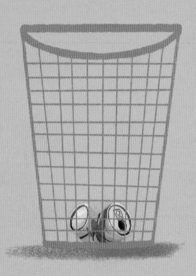

More Little Tiger tales to make you twinkle . . .

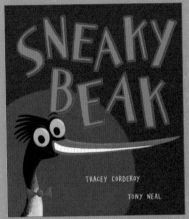

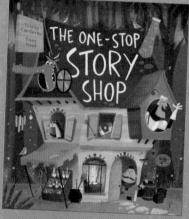

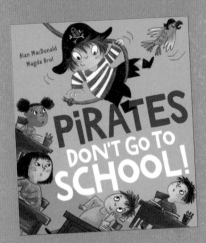

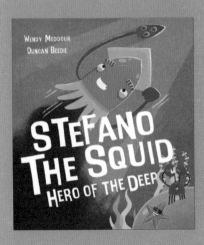